Philippians

30 Daily Insights by **David Sanford**

Our Daily Bread Publishing is affiliated
with Our Daily Bread Ministries.

Requests for permission to quote
from this book should be directed to:
Permissions Department
Our Daily Bread Publishing
P.O. Box 3566
Grand Rapids, MI 49501
Or contact us by email at
permissionsdept@dhp.org

Design by Joshua Tan
Typeset by Grace Goh

ISBN 978-1-913135-30-0

Printed in the United Kingdom

Foreword

Today we begin a 30-day adventure through one of the most beloved New Testament epistles. Why does the apostle Paul write this letter to the believers in Philippi? Seven reasons stand out.

First, he has a strong love for them as their spiritual father (Philippians 1:1–11).

Second, he is confident that God will allow him to visit them again (vv. 12–26).

Third, he has a deep concern that personal disagreements between certain individuals might divide the church and damage its witness—unless those individuals become Christ-centred again (1:27–2:18; 4:2–9).

Fourth, he wants to encourage the Philippian church to warmly welcome Timothy, who will be visiting them again soon, though probably without Paul this time (2:19–24).

Fifth, he wants them to welcome back their brother Epaphroditus, who risked his life to help Paul on their behalf (vv. 25–30).

Sixth, he is troubled that ungodly men are trying to lead them away from the trust in Jesus Christ that he, Paul, had taught and modelled for them on previous visits (3:1–4:1).

Last but not least, he wants to express his joy and gratitude for their prayers and financial support for his ministry as an apostle to the Gentiles (4:10–23).

These seven reasons may seem diverse, but if we look at them carefully, they all relate to one overarching reason why Paul sits down to write this epistle to the Philippians: he simply loves them.

David Sanford

We're glad you've decided to join us on a journey into a deeper relationship with Jesus Christ!

For over 50 years, we have been known for our daily Bible reading notes, *Our Daily Bread*. Many readers enjoy the pithy, inspiring, and relevant articles that point them to God and the wisdom and promises of His unchanging Word.

Building on the foundation of *Our Daily Bread*, we have developed this *Journey Through* series to help believers spend time with God in His Word, book by book. We trust this daily meditation on God's Word will draw you into a closer relationship with Him through our Lord and Saviour, Jesus Christ.

How to use this resource

READ: This book is designed to be read alongside God's Word as you journey with Him. It offers explanatory notes to help you understand the Scriptures in fresh ways.

REFLECT: The questions are designed to help you respond to God and His Word, letting Him change you from the inside out.

RECORD: The space provided allows you to keep a diary of your journey as you record your thoughts and jot down your responses.

An Overview

The most joy-filled of all New Testament letters, Paul's epistle to the Philippians offers many counter-intuitive, heavenly-minded insights into life on earth. The more time we spend in this letter and allow its truths to shape our lives, the more joyful we will become.

When the apostle writes this letter to the followers of Jesus Christ in the city of Philippi, what is on his mind? His suffering and imprisonment for the gospel? Not at all! Paul is more concerned about the Philippian believers than himself. He encourages them to recognise God's work among them and to live in unity, pleasing God and being Christ-like, so that he may rejoice in their growth when he visits them again. (Already, his co-worker Timothy is planning to see them again. Before that, one of their own, Epaphroditus, will bring this letter.)

Sadly, false teachers have shaken the church while others apparently have left because of their godlessness. Paul does not want this to discourage or divide the believers. Instead, he encourages them to keep going strong in the Lord, just as they have been doing since the church's initial founding. What he says will encourage us, too!

The Structure of Philippians

1:1–11	Personal greetings and prayers
1:12–26	Living for Jesus Christ, no matter what happens
1:27–2:30	Loving Jesus Christ and others in all situations
3:1–4:1	Staying true to Christ and rejecting false religiosity
4:2–9	Embracing love, harmony, joy, peace, and purity
4:10–23	Thanksgiving, promises, greetings, and blessings

Key Verse

"For to me, to live is Christ and to die is gain." —Philippians 1:21

Day 1

Read Philippians 1:1–2

Do you have close Christian friends who live far away? If you do, how does it feel when you receive a warmly-worded text, heartfelt letter, or joyful call from them? In a word: *Blessed!*

Several years have passed since Paul, Silas, Luke, and Timothy first visited the city of Philippi (Acts 16:12–40). The congregation is now perhaps a decade old and, in many ways, a noteworthy example of a New Testament church. As an interesting aside, many Bible scholars believe that Luke stayed behind and served as the church's spiritual leader during its infancy. Thus, part of the credit for the thriving church, humanly speaking, goes to Luke, while the other part goes to the overseers and deacons (Philippians 1:1).

Not only has the Philippian church grown spiritually, it has also grown numerically. The initial nucleus of believers included Lydia, the city jailer and his family, and a young woman freed from demon possession. It also included Clement, Euodia, and Syntyche, who worked shoulder to shoulder with Paul (4:2–3). From that small group, an established church has developed.

Paul starts by blessing the Philippian believers: "Grace and peace to you from God our Father and the Lord Jesus Christ" (1:2). The first blessing, "grace", appears twice in the opening chapter (vv. 2, 7) and a third time in the letter's closing verse (4:23). In the context of the greetings in chapter 1, grace speaks of God's eternal riches and infinite goodness, freely given to us. How good it is that we can thank God daily for bringing us into His family! And how good it is that we can enjoy grace-filled relationships with each other! When we reconcile with a fellow believer, that is God's grace at work.

The second blessing, "peace", appears once here (1:2) and twice in the closing chapter (4:7, 9). In this context, peace speaks of the calmness, assurance, and joy we experience when we enter God's presence through prayer. That's when we give Him thanks for who He is, what He has done for us through Christ, and what He has promised to do for us.

God's peace is not dependent on our circumstances in life. Even in prison, Paul feels deeply blessed—so much so that he can extend God's grace and peace to others.

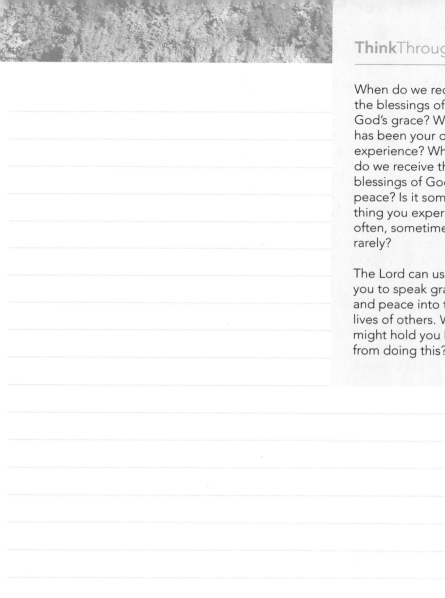

When do we receive the blessings of God's grace? What has been your own experience? When do we receive the blessings of God's peace? Is it something you experience often, sometimes, or rarely?

The Lord can use you to speak grace and peace into the lives of others. What might hold you back from doing this?

Day 2

Read Philippians 1:3–8

In the opening verses of this joy-filled New Testament epistle, we find Paul repeatedly expressing deep feelings of joy and love for the Philippian believers (1:3, 4, 7, 8).

This close bond is noteworthy, particularly when we consider that Paul and the recipients of this letter, the Philippian church, were separated by more than 1,100 kilometres. In the ancient world, such a distance would have made communication difficult. Also, some of Paul's readers would not have spent much time with him, while some might not have even met the apostle.

Despite this, a remarkably strong bond unites Paul with his readers. He loves them, he offers wonderful prayers for them, and he thanks God for them. Likewise, the Philippian believers have great affection for Paul. They pray for him through thick and thin (v. 19), and when possible, provide financial support to the often hard-pressed apostle (2:25; 4:10, 14–18).

It is important that we take note of the Philippian church's "partnership in the gospel from the first day until now" (1:5). Theirs was a partnership that was substantive, heartfelt, and dedicated. No other church, especially in those early days, came anywhere close to doing the same (4:15).

What joyfully bonds Paul to the Philippian church, and vice versa? It's the gospel of Jesus Christ—the very power of God to save us, to seal our shared destiny, to unite us in this life, and to keep us together no matter what happens (or doesn't happen) this side of heaven. **Paul is joyfully confident that God will complete the good work He has started in the Philippian church until the day of Christ Jesus (1:6).**

This gospel continues to create lasting bonds of love and friendship between believers today. How wonderful that we can still share the same bonds of joy with other believers that Paul had with these early brothers and sisters in Christ!

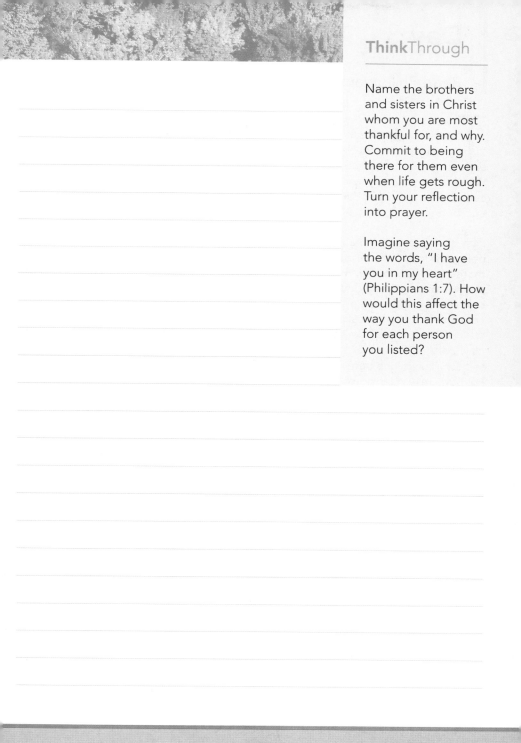

Name the brothers
and sisters in Christ
whom you are most
thankful for, and why.
Commit to being
there for them even
when life gets rough.
Turn your reflection
into prayer.

Imagine saying
the words, "I have
you in my heart"
(Philippians 1:7). How
would this affect the
way you thank God
for each person
you listed?

Day 3

Read Philippians 1:9–11

Today, we receive great encouragement to keep going strong for the Lord. The encouragement in these verses comes in the form of a prayer, which we too can pray for our Christian friends—and ourselves.

First, Paul prays that the Philippian believers' love "may abound more and more" (1:9). Of course, this isn't "love" as the world typically defines it—a calculated love based on personal convenience or physical (or other) desirability. It is the love that God gives us (1 John 4:19)—an unconditional and self-sacrificing love demonstrated by His Son, Jesus Christ, when He died on the cross for us. **In response to this love, we love Him and show heartfelt, practical, and prayerful love for others.**

Second, Paul prays that their love will grow "in knowledge and depth of insight" (Philippians 1:9). God's love within us isn't vague or vaporous. It is tangible, experiential, and life-changing. God's love isn't based on knowing profound somethings, but is based on knowing the greatest Someone. Indeed, God is Someone we can spend our whole lives getting to know better. We can do that consciously and daily by surrendering to the Holy Spirit who dwells within us—and by keeping in step with Him (Galatians 5:25).

Third, Paul's prayer indicates that a growing love will enable the Philippian church to "discern what is best" and "be pure and blameless for the day of Christ" (Philippians 1:10). The value of discernment is two-fold. One, growing in God's love helps us understand what really matters, which is enjoying purity of heart and life. Two, practising God's love towards others helps us focus on what really matters, which is encouraging them to also enjoy purity of heart and life.

Finally, Paul prays for the believers to be "filled with the fruit of righteousness that comes through Jesus Christ" (v. 11). What an excellent prayer this is! Today, we tend to pray primarily for physical or practical needs. Let's follow Paul's example of putting the spiritual needs of others high on our prayer lists.

Take time to pray
Paul's prayer for
yourself. Which of
his points seems
the most pertinent
to you?

What struggles do
you face in prayer?
Bring them to the
Lord and ask Him to
ignite a passion for
prayer within you.

Day 4

Read Philippians 1:12–18

Paul is probably under prolonged house arrest in Rome as he writes this epistle (Acts 28:16). He is guarded around the clock.

Worse, troublemakers are stirring things up for him while he is in chains (Philippians 1:17). These troublemakers aren't necessarily people out to defame Jesus Christ and His gospel; they may be jealous preachers trying to steal the limelight while Paul is confined.

Given these circumstances, it would be understandable if Paul is discouraged. But he remains joyful. He says, "what has happened to me has actually served to advance the gospel" (v. 12). Then he goes on to present three counter-intuitive, heavenly-minded reasons for saying this.

First, Paul has a constant stream of Roman soldiers with whom he can share Jesus Christ. As a result, they have learnt about the gospel and have talked about it with the rest of the palace guard and everyone else (v. 13). Even in today's world, word of mouth is still the most effective way to reach the masses.

Second, Paul's imprisonment has caused a number of godly Christians to "become confident in the Lord and dare all the more to proclaim the gospel without fear" (v. 14). Only the empowering of the Holy Spirit (Acts 1:8) can make people fearless in doing God's good and perfect will, despite danger and possible imprisonment. And like Paul, they will be motivated by love (Philippians 1:16)—for God and for him.

Third, a growing percentage of the region's population has learnt about Jesus Christ (v. 18). The more fiery the hypocrites and the fiercer the critics, the more God is glorified. **Since God wants everyone to hear the good news, He can and will use anything and anyone to communicate it.** The next time you hear an unusual testimony about someone coming to Jesus Christ—for example, someone coming to faith after noticing an atheist's Facebook comment, reading a secular article, or listening to a worldly song—remember Paul's words here and rejoice (v. 18).

Whatever our circumstances, let's always look for heavenly-minded reasons to rejoice and give thanks in Jesus Christ.

Is there someone
who is an example
and encouragement
for you to share the
gospel? Pray for
them, their witness,
and yours.

What is hindering
you from proclaim-
ing Jesus Christ in
the face of danger or
suffering?

Day 5

Read Philippians 1:19–26

Imagine that you have been arrested because of your obedience to God, and now await execution. Would you struggle with the question, "Lord, am I ready to die for you?" Today, we will examine Paul's bold response to this question.

In a few years, Paul will be martyred. Yet, when writing to the Philippian church, he seems confident that he will be released (1:19; 2:24). Regardless, Paul has already decided on his life goals—he knows that to live is Christ and to die is gain (1:21). He is ready to die for Christ. Let's study his mindset.

First, Paul says "I will in no way be ashamed" (v. 20). This means he is determined not to display cowardice or wilful disobedience. Instead, he is committed to honouring Christ by proclaiming the good news. It is his foremost priority.

Second, Paul expects and hopes that he "will have sufficient courage" (v. 20) to stay true to the Lord. Having been arrested by the Roman authorities, he wants a full measure of courage to live for Christ to the very end. **Proclaiming Christ is far more worthwhile than any of the countless foolhardy and trivial endeavours this world has to offer.** Despite this, society continues to oppose and mock our efforts.

Third, "now as always Christ will be exalted in my body" (v. 20). Paul views his body as an instrument made by God for service to Him. His body bears the marks of beatings and whippings. Despite this, Paul doesn't see service to God as mere duty. His is the high view of ambassadorship and apostolic ministry, and therefore Paul delights in carrying out "fruitful labour" (v. 22) for "your progress and joy in the faith" (v. 25), so that "your boasting in Christ Jesus will abound" (v. 26).

Paul's eyes are fixed on Jesus Christ, and his heart has been reshaped by God for others, despite physical pain and suffering. Let's take a moment to meditate on Paul's commitment to God—and reflect on our own commitment to Him.

Is living for Christ Jesus more of a duty or delight for you? Why?

How should looking forward to seeing Jesus affect the way Christians face death and suffering?

Day 6

Read Philippians 1:27–28

Paul continues his heavenward focus by encouraging the Philippian believers to live "in a manner worthy of the gospel of Christ"—and in particular, to "stand firm in the one Spirit"—amid persecution (1:27). Paul may be offering a general exhortation. Or, he may be addressing specific believers who are in conflict with each other, causing disunity in the church.

Whom might Paul have in mind? Later, he will name names (4:2). For now, know that they are believers who love God, have served faithfully for many years, and yet are struggling to follow Jesus Christ in three important ways.

Their first struggle? To "conduct yourselves in a manner worthy of the gospel of Christ" (1:27). Scripture, church history, modern biographies, and contemporary experience make it abundantly clear that God's people don't always live like God's people. But let's not feel defeated. The key to living worthy lives is acknowledging that through Christ, we have been reconciled to God (Romans 5:18); we have died to ourselves and have risen with Him (Galatians 2:19–20); and we no longer live for our glory, but for His (Romans 14:7–9). If we consciously ask God for the indwelling Holy Spirit to empower us, we can live worthy lives. The choice is ours.

Their second struggle? To "stand firm in the one Spirit, striving together as one for the faith of the gospel" (Philippians 1:27). When we don't live like God's people, we will inevitably experience disunity with other believers. When I'm out of sync with God, I'm automatically out of sync with my brothers and sisters in Christ. Worse, I become contentious and oppositional. Again, we need the Holy Spirit to empower us. Otherwise, division and derision will result.

Their third struggle? Not to be "frightened in any way by those who oppose you" (v. 28). It's bad enough to experience opposition, but it's even worse to face persecution while we're out of sync with God and our fellow Christians. The answer, however, isn't to focus on this third struggle. Rather, it is to address the first two struggles and then ask God for courage. Then we'll stand tall.

Paul's words deserve careful attention. If we are in conflict with other believers, or if we are witnessing such conflict in the church, we need to reflect: How can we conduct ourselves in a manner worthy of the gospel? How can we stand firm in the one Spirit?

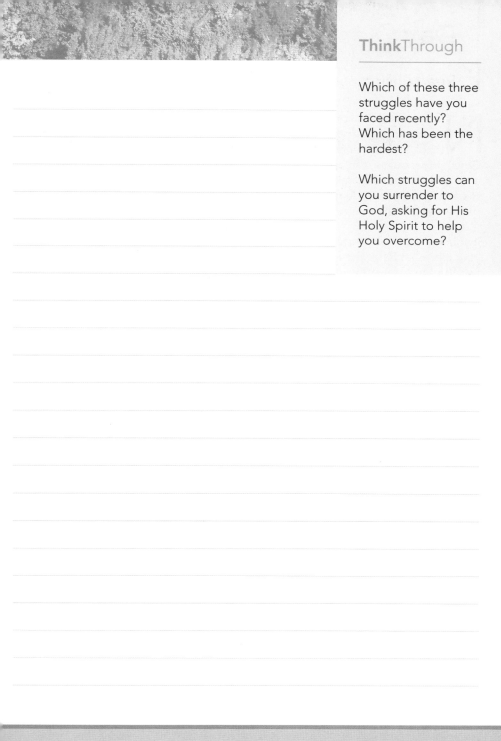

Which of these three struggles have you faced recently? Which has been the hardest?

Which struggles can you surrender to God, asking for His Holy Spirit to help you overcome?

Day 7

Read Philippians 1:29–30

Now that the Philippians have received salvation, they, like Paul, are suffering for Jesus Christ. In response, the apostle offers a number of heavenly-minded insights. His aim is to encourage them to keep persevering in their faith.

If you are experiencing suffering in your life, what Paul says in today's two brief but powerful verses will encourage you and help bring healing. If not, what Paul says will prepare you. Let's look at the insights Paul offers about suffering for Jesus Christ.

Paul points out that suffering "has been granted to you" (Philippians 1:29) by God from eternity past. Our suffering in this life never takes God by surprise; we have the privilege of identifying with our Lord and Saviour (Acts 9:16; 14:22; Philippians 3:8–10; 1 Thessalonians 3:3; 1 Peter 2:21).

Paul says that such suffering is "on behalf of Christ" (Philippians 1:29) and is for His glory, honour, and praise. Our suffering for Christ on earth, whether due to opposition or persecution—for example, when we face derision for praying in public or saying "Merry Christmas"—always has a divine purpose (Romans 5:3–5; James 1:2–4; 1 Peter 1:6–9; 4:16).

"Not only to believe in him, but also to suffer for him" (Philippians 1:29). When we put our faith in Jesus Christ, we are saved now and for eternity. Our suffering on earth is real but temporary. Our future joy is even more real because it is eternal (Romans 8:28–30; 2 Corinthians 1:9; 4:16–18; 1 Peter 4:12–14). Both now and later, our suffering for Jesus Christ is always for something—for the Lord's sake (Isaiah 48:10; Ephesians 5:26–27; Titus 2:14).

Paul reassures his readers that they are not alone in undergoing trials—it is "the same struggle you saw I had, and now hear that I still have" (Philippians 1:30). Our suffering is no different from what others have faced (Deuteronomy 8:5; Proverbs 3:11–12; Hebrews 12:6–11; 1 Peter 5:1); no one is exempt. Our suffering, however, is eased by the godly example of others (2 Corinthians 1:3–7; 12:8–10; Hebrews 11:32–40; 12:1; James 5:10–11; 1 Peter 5:9). In addition, our steadfastness in the face of suffering displays the truth of our redemption to a watching world (John 9:3; 11:4; 1 Peter 2:11–12; 3:13–15).

How can Paul's insights about suffering for Jesus Christ help you face suffering differently?

Consider the examples of Christ (Hebrews 12:3–4) and Paul. How can you be an example to others too?

Day 8

Read Philippians 2:1–4

In today's passage, Paul expounds on the importance of walking in *unity*. He then advocates *humility*—namely, concern for others' needs and not just one's own—as the basis for that unity (Philippians 1:22–26).

So, how do we demonstrate humility, show concern for the needs of others, and thereby strengthen unity in our local churches? Paul lists four ways.

The first way is by "being like-minded" (2:2). This means we're in sync with God and our fellow believers. We're filled with God's love. We're joyfully filled with the Holy Spirit. We're happy to encourage others. We're glad to show much grace. Let's be determined to make this our daily experience.

The second way is by "having the same love" (v. 2) for your fellow believers as you have for God. This is hardest to do in times of suffering, as pain causes us to turn inward. In such times, many of us long to feel a tangible embrace from God, to know He is with us and cares. In such times, we are unable or unwilling to be there for other people and care for them. **Yet what more could Jesus Christ do than He already has done on Calvary?** Yes, that's right: He ascended back to heaven and now offers specific, heartfelt prayers for each of us by name. What comfort

and love, indeed! Now, let's share that comfort and love with our fellow believers (2 Corinthians 1:3–7).

The third way is by "being one in spirit and of one mind" (Philippians 2:2). After His ascension, Jesus sent the Holy Spirit to *all* believers. While the Spirit's indwelling is permanent, His filling isn't. This is why we need to ask God daily to fill us with and govern us by His Spirit (see Ephesians 5:18). Like Christ, the Spirit is our Master, Teacher, and Leader. He not only fills every fibre of our being, but also speaks directly to us. Are we listening? If so, we enjoy sweet fellowship with the Spirit.

The fourth way is to "in humility value others above yourselves", "looking . . . to the interests of the others" (Philippians 2:3–4) as you make choices each day. Again, the Spirit makes this possible at every turn. After all, He is our constant Comforter, Counsellor, and Encourager. True, when we sin, He is grieved. And when we keep sinning, He is quenched. But when we ask God to wash and cleanse us, the Spirit is ready to fill us anew. The Spirit speaks words of tenderness and compassion. All is forgiven. All is renewed. Now, demonstrate humility, show concern for the needs of others, and thereby strengthen the unity within your church.

Which one of the four ways described in Philippians 2:1–4 comes easiest for you?

Which one of these four ways comes hardest for you?

Day 9

Read Philippians 2:5–8

Even though I've read the book of Philippians hundreds of times, my voice shook as I re-read today's Scripture passage aloud.

"Have the same mindset as Christ Jesus," Paul writes (Philippians 2:5). He then goes on to quote an early Christian poem or hymn of praise to Jesus Christ.

Paul's aim is to encourage his readers to be united by having a heart of humility, like Christ himself. That's why he points out the humility of Jesus Christ: to ask the Philippians to relate to each other in a similar fashion.

As you read this passage, ask God to move your heart, as He moved mine.

First, be deeply moved by Jesus Christ's standing within the Trinity. He is God the Son and therefore "in very nature God" (v. 6). There has never been a gap between Jesus' full deity and the full deity of God the Father. There has never been anything for Jesus to prove, seek, or attain. From eternity past to eternity future, He is the King of kings and Lord of lords. All He had to do to create the heavens and earth was merely speak the word.

What's more, the Lord Jesus came to earth, often. As the second Person in the Trinity, He walked in the Garden of Eden with Adam and Eve (Genesis 3:8). He appeared and spoke to Enoch, Noah, Abraham and Sarah, Isaac and Rebekah, Jacob and Rachel, Joseph, and many others (John 8:56–58). The prophet Isaiah saw Him (John 12:41), trembled, and rejoiced. Throughout ancient history, He prophesied the first and second Advents (Luke 24:25–48).

Second, be deeply moved by Jesus Christ's identification with humanity. He didn't come just to meet some of the great heroes of the faith. Instead, he "made himself nothing" (Philippians 2:7). This was no short, holiday visit. Instead, he was born in a borrowed Bethlehem manger (Luke 2:7). He knew what it was like to be a refugee, a child whisked across political borders (Matthew 2:13–15, 19–23). He grew up in a God-fearing household with many siblings. He served as a carpenter until age 30 (Matthew 13:55; Mark 6:3; Luke 3:23). He maintained a pure and holy life, without sin (Hebrews 4:15).

Ultimately, "he humbled himself by becoming obedient to death—even death on a cross!" (Philippians 2:8). Let us pause here and meditate: in our dealings, decisions, mindset, and behaviour, are we imitators of Jesus Christ? In our relationships with one another, are we humble like Christ?

What about Jesus Christ moves you the most? How can you best praise the Lord for who He is and what He has done?

Read Matthew 16:24. How does Jesus' example of humility—and making himself nothing—inspire you to conduct yourself differently in your relationships with others?

Day 10

Read Philippians 2:9–11

How good that the cross and grave aren't the end of the story. Far from it!

On the third day, Jesus rose from the dead. He appeared to His apostles and many others over a period of 40 days (Matthew 28; Mark 16; Luke 24; John 20–21; Acts 1:3–8). Then, in the presence of the Eleven, He ascended back to heaven (Luke 24:51; Acts 1:2, 9–11; 1 Timothy 3:16). Out of deepest humiliation came greatest exaltation.

God the Father has given Jesus the greatest honour in the universe. One day, every creature "in heaven and on earth and under the earth" (Philippians 2:10) will do two things. First, "every knee [will] bow" (v. 10) in submission to Jesus Christ. Second, everyone will audibly "acknowledge that Jesus Christ is Lord, to the glory of God the Father" (v. 11).

Let's delve into the significance of today's Scripture passage.

The words take us back to 700 BC. In a majestic passage from Isaiah 45:18–24, the LORD (Yahweh) speaks to the nations. He describes himself as Creator of the heavens and earth (v. 18), the one and only LORD God (vv. 18, 21, 22), one who speaks only truth (vv. 19, 23), the only one who knows the future (v. 21), and "a

righteous God and a Saviour"(v. 21). Then the LORD issues these words: "Turn to me and be saved, all you ends of the earth; for I am God, and there is no other. By myself I have sworn, my mouth has uttered in all integrity a word that will not be revoked: before me every knee will bow; by me every tongue will swear" (vv. 22–23).

When Paul writes to the Philippian believers, he is clearly applying this stirring prophecy to Jesus Christ. What's more, he is saying that Jesus is the LORD (Yahweh). (Paul wrote his letter to the Philippians in ancient Greek, which had no equivalent to "Yahweh". But we know he meant that Jesus is Yahweh because "Yahweh" is used explicitly five times in the Isaiah passage he references.)

In the end, the question isn't, "Is Jesus Lord?" He is, now and for eternity. Instead, the question is: "Have you acknowledged that fact in your own life?" **How good it is to gladly acknowledge His place in the universe and in your life and mine, here and now.** As we saw in Philippians 2:5–8, this means that we choose to be humble in our relationships with each other. Such humility and unity greatly honour Jesus as our Lord.

List the major
spheres of your life.
In which do you
need to acknowl-
edge that Jesus
is Lord?

What is one way
you can gladly
acknowledge that
Jesus is Lord
today in a sphere
of your life?

Day 11

Read Philippians 2:12–18

In this epistle, Paul twice addresses the Philippian believers as "dear friends" (2:12–14; 4:1–3). In both instances, he calls on them to end their divisiveness and disunity in order to glorify God—now and in eternity.

How do fellow Christians put an end to divisiveness and disunity? And why should we? The apostle offers six compelling insights.

First, Paul exhorts the Philippians to work out the fruit of their salvation "with fear and trembling" (2:12). God disciplines those who divide His people by grumbling and arguing (Numbers 16:1–50; 1 Corinthians 10:10–12; Jude 11).

Second, Paul says "it is God who works in you to will and to act in order to fulfil his good purpose" (Philippians 2:13). Like Pharaoh, it is possible to rebel against God, create great strife and disunity among His people, suffer great punishment, and still fulfil the *general* purposes of God (Exodus 9:16; Isaiah 14:24–27; 46:10–14; Romans 9:17–21). However, as Christians we are empowered by God to fulfil His *good* purposes by our reverence, holiness, humility, and unity (Romans 8:28; Ephesians 1:9–11; 2 Timothy 1:9).

Third, Paul links the working out of our salvation to the practical exhortation: "do everything without grumbling or arguing" (Philippians 2:14). Sadly, this has been the unresolved sin of some within the Philippian church (4:2). **Unity, agreement, and single-mindedness should characterise all that we do.**

Fourth, the result of not complaining or arguing—and of unity in the church—is "so that you may become blameless and pure, 'children of God without fault in a warped and crooked generation.' Then you will shine among them like stars in the sky as you hold firmly to the word of life" (2:15–16). God's purposes for the Philippian believers are good indeed!

Fifth, Paul links the working out of the church's salvation to his own spiritual journey: "And then I will be able to boast on the day of Christ that I did not run or labour in vain" (v. 16). Among other things, the day of Christ refers to when we see Him in His glory. It also speaks of the final assessment of what we have done on earth.

Finally, Paul wants the day of Christ to be a day of celebration for all (vv. 17–18). Here, he draws the picture of a drink offering (v. 17, see 2 Timothy 4:6–8). Instead of wine, however, the apostle is ready to shed his own blood. For the believer, death is not defeat. Instead, it's the day we meet Jesus Christ face to face.

What produces the
most awe of God in
your life?

In a difficult relation-
ship, which of Paul's
six insights could
help you the most?

Day 12

Read Philippians 2:19–24

Paul has many brothers in Christ, but not many sons. Without question, his foremost son in the faith is Timothy, whose name means "one who honours and respects God" in Greek.

From Acts 16:1–3, we know that Timothy's father is a Greek and his Jewish mother is a strong woman of faith. The churches also speak very highly of Timothy. So, Paul invites Timothy to join him on his second and third missionary journeys (Acts 16–21).

From 2 Timothy, we also learn that Timothy's Jewish grandmother is a strong believer, and that she and her daughter faithfully taught the Scriptures to him from a very young age (1:5; 3:15). In later years, the local churches faithfully taught him the Scriptures too (see Acts 16:2).

The greetings at the beginning of six epistles (2 Corinthians, Philippians, Colossians, 1 and 2 Thessalonians, and Philemon) include Timothy's name after Paul's. It is thought that Paul dictated these epistles to his dear son in the faith, who scribed them down faithfully.

It's no surprise, then, that Paul affirms how "Timothy has proved himself, because as a son with his father he has served with me in the work of the gospel" (Philippians 2:22). Timothy serves shoulder to shoulder with the great apostle year after year in the cause of Christ. If anyone knows Paul's weaknesses, foibles, and failings, it is Timothy. Yet his unshakable loyalty to the Lord and to Paul makes Timothy a man without peer.

How much Timothy means to Paul can hardly be overstated. Paul knows of no one else who is so selfless and passionate about following Jesus Christ and, in particular, who cares so much for the welfare of the Philippian believers. **This suggests that the attention, affection, nurture, and care that Timothy received from infancy to adulthood produced the real deal—a man who loves the Lord wholeheartedly and loves others well.** The Greatest Commandment (Matthew 22:35–40; Mark 12:28–31; Luke 10:25–28) always bears good fruit indeed.

No wonder Paul says, "I have no one else like him" (Philippians 2:20). And no wonder Paul wants to send him to Philippi "as soon as I see how things go with me" (v. 23).

Timothy does not share the same standing or authority as Paul. Yet, what a great man of faith he is in so many ways.

How much does the Greatest Commandment determine the direction and content of your life?

Like Timothy, how can we be more "others-focused" in our leadership or example to other believers?

Read Philippians 2:25–30

The name Epaphroditus means "handsome" and "agreeable". After the near-death illness he experiences (Philippians 2:27), we should probably add "one whom God restored to life".

Epaphroditus is a believer in Christ from Philippi. He had been sent by the Philippian church to take care of Paul's needs, and now Paul has sent him back to the Philippian believers.

Paul expresses his utmost respect for Epaphroditus by calling him "brother, co-worker and fellow soldier" (v. 25). Like Timothy, Epaphroditus loves the Lord wholeheartedly and loves others as himself. Some biblical scholars have concluded that Epaphroditus was likely a risk-taking leader, willing to place himself in harm's way. Others have suggested that he may have been a man of means. Whatever the case, he set out on a journey of well over 1,100 kilometres, carrying generous and valuable gifts for Paul (4:18). "Travel safety" were two words that didn't usually appear together in the ancient world: Epaphroditus faced potential dangers on both land and sea and, like Paul, this probably included hostility from other travellers, soldiers, and bandits.

In the end, Epaphroditus fell dangerously ill and "almost died for the work of Christ . . . [risking] his life to make up for the help you yourselves could not give me" (2:30). It's likely that both Paul and Timothy cared for their brother, prayed for his life, and nursed him back to health.

Epaphroditus' return trip to Philippi would likely have been equally arduous, though this time the treasure he carried was this epistle, written on leather or parchment. This epistle has now been translated into more than 1,520 languages and published billions of times. Today, we can read, understand, reflect, and apply God's Word to the Philippians anew.

No wonder Paul instructed the Philippian believers to "welcome [Epaphroditus] in the Lord with great joy, and honour people like him" (v. 29). Do you know any risk-taking missionaries, church planters, or pastors? If so, how can you demonstrate your respect for these leaders today?

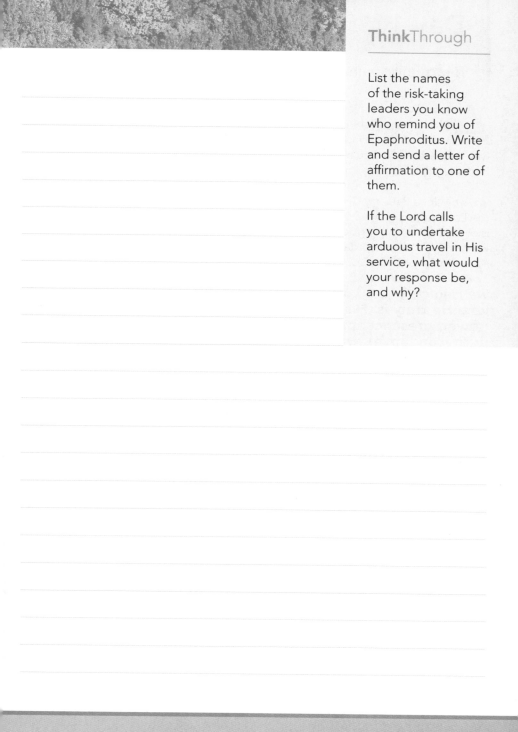

ThinkThrough

List the names of the risk-taking leaders you know who remind you of Epaphroditus. Write and send a letter of affirmation to one of them.

If the Lord calls you to undertake arduous travel in His service, what would your response be, and why?

Day 14

Read Philippians 3:1–3

A world where believers must always be watching out for false teachers and evildoers? That was the case in the ancient world—and sadly, it is also the case today.

So, why does Paul say, "rejoice in the Lord" (Philippians 3:1)? The key is "in the Lord". How good that we can thank the Lord daily for His sovereignty, providence, holiness, love, and mysterious ways. **When we rejoice in the Lord for who He truly is (His infinite power, presence, providence, purity, and love), we will know how to stay true to Jesus Christ and shun false religiosity.**

Therefore, Paul doesn't apologise for warning the Philippian believers again. First, "it is a safeguard for you" (v. 1). Second, it's always time to "watch out" (v. 2). As Christians, we are called to be vigilant at all times.

The early church was beset by Judaizers, who wrongly added Old Testament requirements, like circumcision, to the gospel (Acts 15:1–5; Galatians 2:3-10, 15-16; 5:2–4). Paul compares the Judaizers to dogs (Philippians 3:2). Biblically, this is a term often applied to false teachers and evildoers. Among others,

Jesus includes "those who practise magic arts, the sexually immoral, the murderers, the idolaters and everyone who loves and practises falsehood" (Revelation 22:15). No wonder Paul wants us to watch out.

What, then, is the difference between a false teacher and an evildoer? The latter isn't always a teacher, but the former is always an evildoer (Philippians 3:2), often in the guise of pretentious-spirituality. The Judaizers of Paul's day were "mutilators of the flesh" (v. 2) and false teachers.

Sadly, false teachers and evildoers abound today, in every nation and culture. It's not enough to just watch out. Paul urges us to constantly "serve God by his Spirit" (v. 3), wherever we are, inviting others to do the same (see John 4:23–24). He also urges us to "boast in Christ Jesus" (Philippians 3:3) for His work in our lives, including opportunities to share the faith with others (Romans 15:17–18).

In the face of false teachers, the best antidote for *others*—non-believers—is for us to proclaim the gospel of Christ in word and deed. The best antidote for *us*, as Christians, is rejoicing in the Lord for who He truly is.

Make a list of words and phrases that describe the Lord. Use it to thank God for who He truly is.

Can you think of someone who is teaching wrong doctrine? Pray and ask God to touch his heart and open his eyes to the truth.

Day 15

Read Philippians 3:4–6

One of my mentors has repeatedly warned me over 35 years: "Beware the man who always thinks he is right." **Being convinced you are always right is a dangerous form of pretentious-spirituality.** No man or woman is always right; only God is always right.

That's why Paul doesn't simply urge us to "put no confidence in the flesh" (Philippians 3:3); he also describes how he had persecuted early Christians as a result of his own pretentious-spirituality.

Before his radical conversion, Paul thought he was always right. Under the name Saul (his Jewish name), he cultivated and flaunted his impeccable pedigree.

At a moment's notice, Paul lists his pedigree's seven perfections, which he once considered vital to who he was. First, he was "circumcised on the eighth day" (v. 5) as prescribed in the Law. Second, he is "of the people of Israel" (v. 5), meaning he is not tainted by Gentile blood. Third, he is "of the tribe of Benjamin" (v. 5), the tribe most loyal to the monarchy of old. Fourth, he is "a Hebrew of Hebrews" (v. 5) in language, thought, and life. Fifth, he was "in regard to the law, a Pharisee" (v. 5), meaning he was orthodox in every way. Sixth and

seventh, he emphasises the details of his "perfect" life: "as for zeal, persecuting the church" (v. 6), and "as for righteousness based on the law, faultless" (v. 6) among his peers.

The first three "perfections" were inherited. Saul himself had done nothing to deserve or earn them. The fourth was partially inherited, partially learnt (see Acts 22:3), and partially polished to a pretentiously-spiritual degree by Saul himself. In the end, Saul rejected the moderation of his teacher, Gamaliel (5:34), and became convinced that his orthodoxy and legalistic righteousness surpassed that of his Pharisaic peers. He alone knew what had to be done and had the courage to do it. The stoning of Stephen was the final catalyst, as Saul became a bloodthirsty exterminator of Christian men and women (8:3; 9:1–2; 26:10).

How did Saul become so pretentiously spiritual and bloodthirsty? He imagined he was an exceedingly righteous man, ready to do whatever it took to protect his religion and way of life.

In Saul's mind, the day for trying to convert Christians back to Judaism was long gone. Instead, he thought it was time for slaughter. How good that Jesus Christ personally intervened in Saul's life. All thanks to Christ, the former chief persecutor became the

chief preacher of the good news throughout the ancient Roman Empire. What hope his conversion offers even today.

ThinkThrough

Make a list of people who persecute Christians today.

Boldly ask God to radically convert today's persecutors into tomorrow's evangelists, missionaries, and church planters.

Read Philippians 3:7–11

t's not enough for Paul to warn against false teachers and evildoers. It's not even enough for him to confess his own pretentious-spirituality and bloodthirstiness (before he became a follower of Jesus). At one time, Paul greatly valued his impeccable religious pedigree (Philippians 3:7), but now, "I consider everything a loss" (v. 8).

After considering everything "garbage" (v. 8), Paul exchanges his confidence in his religious pedigree and the law for a confidence in Jesus Christ on the basis of faith (v. 9). This ultimate exchange began the day he put his trust in Jesus Christ as his Lord and Saviour (v. 9)—and it continues as Paul's life in Christ is worked out on a daily basis.

What does each new day in Christ offer Paul? It is this: "The surpassing worth of knowing Christ Jesus my Lord" (v. 8). **It's not enough to meet the Saviour; Paul also wants to fall more and more in love with Him.**

How does Paul want to know Christ better? He lists three ways:

First, Paul wants to know "the power of [Christ's] resurrection" (v. 10). In Romans 1:4, the apostle identifies that power with "the Spirit of holiness" through whom the Son of God was appointed "in power by his resurrection from the dead". He also identifies that power with the life-transforming gospel of salvation (1:16). God's power alone helps us grasp Jesus Christ's infinite love for us. And God's power alone will raise us from the dead and clothe us in new, immortal bodies forever.

Second, Paul wants to participate in Christ's sufferings, "becoming like him in his death" (Philippians 3:10). He connects suffering for the gospel with God's power (2 Timothy 1:8), which made it possible for the twelve apostles to rejoice "because they had been counted worthy of suffering disgrace for the Name" of Jesus (Acts 5:41). Instead of instilling shame or despair, suffering offers the promise of future glory (Romans 8:17).

Third, Paul wants to "[attain] to the resurrection from the dead" (Philippians 3:11). With courage, he repeatedly declares that he stands on trial because of the hope of "the resurrection of the dead" (Acts 23:6; 24:21). Paul looks forward to a physical resurrection like that of Jesus, in a glorified human body (Romans 6:5). As we finish today's devotion, let's take a moment to reflect: Do we long to know Christ Jesus in the three ways Paul did?

God's power enables us to grasp Jesus' love for us and to remain fearless in the face of opposition. What do you need God's power for today?

Are you willing to suffer for Jesus Christ? If so, for what reasons?

Day 17

Read Philippians 3:12–14

To ward off any future temptation towards pretentious-spirituality, Paul declares that obtaining "the surpassing worth of knowing Christ Jesus" (Philippians 3:8) is a daily process. **We'll never fully know Christ this side of eternity; it's a lifelong pursuit.** If this is true for Paul, it's certainly true for you and me.

First, Paul says: "Not that I have already obtained all this, or have already arrived at my goal" (v. 12). When Jesus calls us to "be perfect, therefore, as your heavenly Father is perfect" (Matthew 5:48), He isn't talking about an accomplishment to achieve, but an ultimate goal to pursue.

Elsewhere, Paul calls us to "be transformed by the renewing of your mind. Then you will be able to test and approve what God's will is—his good, pleasing and perfect will" (Romans 12:2). Again, this is aspirational—a daily pursuit and not a once-and-for-all plateau.

The same is true when Paul writes: "Since we have these promises, dear friends, let us purify ourselves from everything that contaminates body and spirit, perfecting holiness out of reverence for God" (2 Corinthians 7:1). He doesn't say, "Permanently protect yourselves once-for-all from everything that contaminates"; it's a process.

Second, Paul says: "I press on to take hold of that for which Christ Jesus took hold of me" (Philippians 3:12). In the New Testament, only Jesus and Paul use the expression, "I press on" (Luke 13:33; Philippians 3:12, 14). In the Old Testament, the expression "press on" appears in Hosea 6:3. This suggests that they know exactly what they are after, and plan to pursue it with utmost determination, steadfastness, and endurance.

How do we press on? The author of Hebrews says we need to "throw off everything that hinders and the sin that so easily entangles". Then we need to fix "our eyes on Jesus, the pioneer and perfecter of faith" (Hebrews 12:1–2).

Third, Paul says: "I press on towards the goal to win the prize for which God has called me heavenwards in Christ Jesus" (Philippians 3:14). The apostle has no intention of slowing down, slipping away, or giving up. Instead, he imagines himself leaning into the finish line and receiving the prize.

For Paul, the finish line is either martyrdom or Jesus Christ's return. Regardless, he plans to enter glory with joy.

What is causing you to slow down, slip away, or give up on pressing on and ultimately receiving the eternal prize? Surrender it to God and follow Paul's example.

Does the impossibility of achieving perfection this side of heaven encourage or discourage you? Why?

Day 18

Read Philippians 3:15–19

Today, Paul appeals to the Philippian believers to make the very best choice. Let's find out what it is.

First, he tells them that, "All of us, then, who are mature should take such a view of things" (Philippians 3:15). Paul is appealing to them to agree with all he has said so far. He is confident that mature Christians will agree with his insights on joy, unity, and love.

Second, he adds, "And if on some point you think differently, that too God will make clear to you" (v. 15). In other words, Paul is confident the Holy Spirit will speak to the heart of anyone who disagrees with his insights. After all, the Holy Spirit is inspiring this letter and gladly wants to illuminate us (1 John 2:20–29).

Third, Paul says, "Only let us live up to what we have already attained" (Philippians 3:16). Again, the idea is to press on instead of changing course or losing ground.

Fourth, he advises, "Join together in following my example, brothers and sisters, and just as you have us as a model, keep your eyes on those who live as we do" (v. 17). Ultimately, we follow Jesus Christ. Practically, however, we follow those who follow Christ (1 Corinthians 11:1), as their examples are tangible, observable, and knowable (2 Thessalonians 3:7).

From the four points Paul makes, it is clear that he longs for the Philippian believers to follow his teachings and godly example. He believes that this would be the best choice for them.

The apostle then tearfully recalls something he warned them about earlier: "many live as enemies of the cross of Christ" (Philippians 3:18). They oppose the gospel, reject Jesus Christ as Lord and Saviour, and do all they can to destroy genuine followers of Christ.

Paul condemns these enemies in the strongest terms (see 2 Peter 2:1–22; Jude 3–16), saying that "their destiny is destruction" (Philippians 3:19). This means they will be sent to hell by God. He also says that "their god is their stomach" (v. 19)—meaning that they worship their evil desires—and "their glory is in their shame" (v. 19). Truly, "their mind is set on earthly things" (v. 19).

Let us not be overwhelmed by the enemies of Jesus Christ. Instead, let us heed the godly, grace-filled examples of true followers of Jesus Christ, which offer rich encouragement, strength, joy, and peace in our own lives every day.

Do you have friends or acquaintances who live as enemies of Christ? Ask God to radically convert each one.

Who provides the best example for you in following Christ wholeheartedly?

Read Philippians 3:20–4:1

Paul offers many assurances to the Philippian believers. They offer comfort, encouragement, and hope to us as well.

The first assurance: "But our citizenship is in heaven" (Philippians 3:20). We have received God's gifts of faith, salvation, and eternal life. We have changed our allegiance. We know, love, serve, and obey the Lord alone.

Some of my friends hold dual citizenships. Some of my relatives used to have these too, but eventually chose to become the citizen of only one country. No matter what our citizenship status is on earth, our heavenly citizenship is much more real, and it reflects our true identity.

The second assurance: "And we eagerly await a Saviour from there, the Lord Jesus Christ" (v. 20). Paul reminds us that as believers, we have a single devotion. We love Christ, we live for Him, and we look forward to spending eternity with Him in the new heaven and new earth.

Many of my friends live in other nations around the world. It is hard to be far apart, and we long to see each other again. Even if we haven't seen each other in months or even years, love binds our hearts. How much stronger is the bond of love we share with Jesus Christ. We long to see Him—and we have the blessed assurance that we will!

The third assurance: "By the power that enables him to bring everything under his control, [Jesus Christ] will transform our lowly bodies so that they will be like his glorious body" (v. 21). Each of us has the incredible promise that Christ will give us a glorious body like His own. In the meantime, our earthly bodies will continue to age, diminish, and eventually perish.

While writing this book, I learnt that my lung disease, which has already cut many years off my projected life span, has infiltrated my heart. My cardiac sarcoidosis could remain status quo for many years. If it progresses to stage three, however, I have a 50-percent chance of dying within a year.

In this context, this third assurance means more to me than ever before. Instead of despairing, I continue to thank the Lord daily for His sovereignty, providence, holiness, love, and mysterious ways. **In Christ, our lives are planned. They have purpose, as well as a glorious and eternal future. What more could we want?**

Read John 3:16,
John 20:30–31, and
1 John 5:13. On a
scale from 1 (lowest)
to 10 (highest), how
certain are you of
going to heaven
when you die?

In what ways
can Paul's three
assurances help
you "stand firm
in the Lord"
(Philippians 4:1)?

Read Philippians 4:2–3

Paul's letter was very likely read out to the Philippian believers, who would have gathered together to listen to it. That's how letters were communicated in those days.

As such, I invite you to picture how today's verses might have been read out to the Philippians. Imagine yourself as one of the believers. The reader of the letter pauses, and you look at Euodia, then at Syntyche. In unguarded moments, the eyes and face reveal one's heart. What do you see? The knowing look of pretentious-spirituality? Or the Spirit-softened look of humility?

As the reader of the letter starts reading out today's verses, his own facial features soften. His eyes begin to water, and his tone of voice changes. "I plead . . ." he begins, and pauses again. Paul rarely uses the word "plead", but he uses it here in rapid succession. "I plead with Euodia and I plead with Syntyche . . ." Silence falls over the room. The congregation takes a collective breath. ". . . to be of the same mind in the Lord" (Philippians 4:2).

The reader continues: "Yes, and I ask you, my true companion [likely Epaphroditus], help these women since they have contended at my side in the cause of the gospel . . ." (v. 3). He pauses again, this time to motion for both women to come forward.

In heaven, everyone will be reconciled, but there is no need to wait that long.

". . . along with Clement and the rest of my co-workers, whose names are in the book of life" (v. 3). Epaphroditus motions to Clement. In turn, Clement motions to a few others, and together, they join Euodia and Syntyche up front. Without a word, the women embrace in tears. All is forgiven. Unity is restored. Clement offers a heartfelt prayer of thanksgiving. Then, they quietly return to their seats.

Wouldn't it be wonderful to meet Euodia and Syntyche in heaven? Maybe we'll get to hear from them about this moment, when today's two verses were read aloud for the first time in Philippi. How deeply moving that would be.

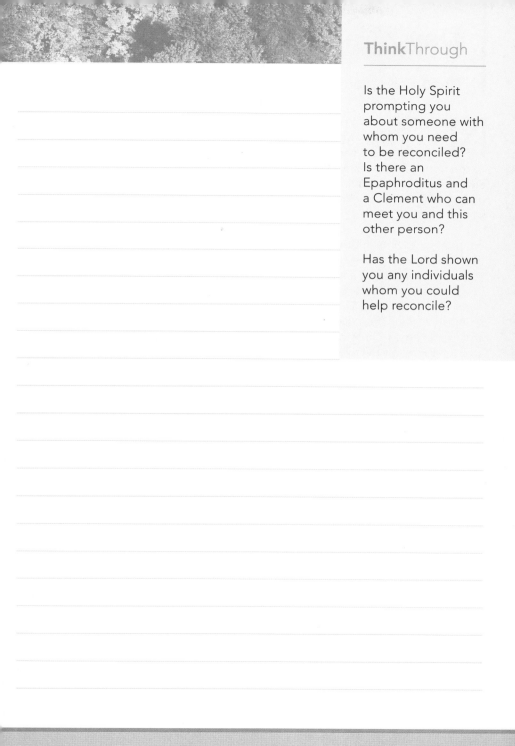

Is the Holy Spirit
prompting you
about someone with
whom you need
to be reconciled?
Is there an
Epaphroditus and
a Clement who can
meet you and this
other person?

Has the Lord shown
you any individuals
whom you could
help reconcile?

Read Philippians 4:4

Now, Paul offers a rapid-fire series of encouraging verses. This first one is short and easy to memorise: "Rejoice in the Lord always. I will say it again: rejoice!" (Philippians 4:4). Let's consider what it says *thematically*.

For the eighth time in this epistle, Paul uses the phrase, "in the Lord". When we rejoice *in the Lord*, it means we have heavenly-minded confidence, hope, and endurance. Throughout his epistles, Paul often speaks of faith and love in Jesus Christ, as well as love for our fellow believers. To rejoice in the Lord, we need to remain in Christ, which leads to loving our fellow believers (John 15:9–12, Colossians 1:4).

Day in and day out, our thoughts, attitudes, words, and actions are either "in the Lord" or not. The latter is the default because of our sinful nature. The former is far and away the best. Each time, it's our choice.

For the second time in this epistle, Paul uses the even more wonderful phrase, "rejoice in the Lord". In Philippians 3:1, he uses this phrase to introduce a chapter full of exhortations to stay true to Jesus Christ (v. 3), to keep pressing on to receive our eternal reward (vv. 12–14), to actively keep following the godly example of Paul and others (v. 17), and to quickly resolve issues and live in harmony with other believers (4:1–3).

Here in Philippians 4:4, Paul uses the phrase "rejoice in the Lord" to introduce a rapid series of encouraging commands to bear with others (v. 5), remember the Lord is near (v. 5), not worry (v. 6), pray about everything (v. 6), experience God's deep and abiding peace (v. 7), think about what is good and right and best (v. 8), be content in every circumstance (v. 12), and ask Jesus to empower us in all things (v. 13).

Our thoughts, attitudes, words, and actions are either "[rejoicing] in the Lord" or not. The former isn't merely a choice; it's to become our way of life. Paul highlights this when he points out that we are to rejoice in the Lord "always" (v. 4).

With the Holy Spirit's empowering, rejoicing and giving thanks to God can truly become our way of life. In Ephesians 5:20, Paul ends by saying, "always giving thanks to God the Father for everything, in the name of our Lord Jesus Christ." Of course, "always" can happen only when the Lord is your first love!

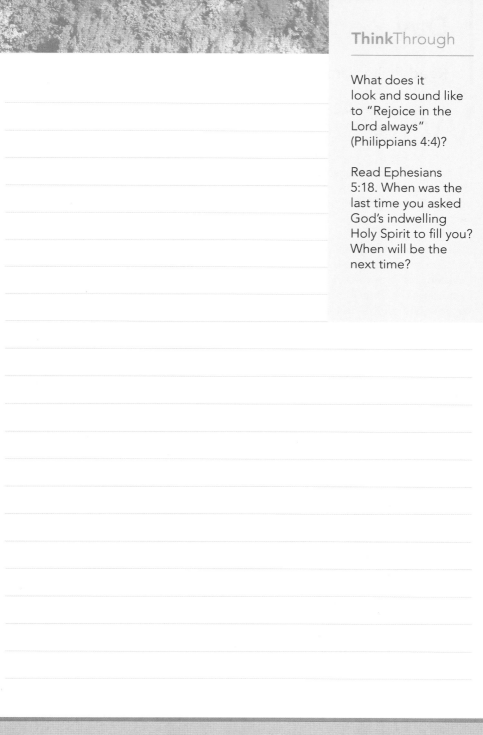

What does it
look and sound like
to "Rejoice in the
Lord always"
(Philippians 4:4)?

Read Ephesians
5:18. When was the
last time you asked
God's indwelling
Holy Spirit to fill you?
When will be the
next time?

Day 22

When Christians memorise Philippians 4:4 and the verses that follow, some may be tempted to skip or gloss over verse 5. That would be a huge mistake. This verse revolutionised my life a few years ago. Let's consider each phrase of this verse in turn.

Paul asks the Philippians to "let your gentleness be evident to all" (v. 5). "Evident" isn't a word we use every day. The New International Version (NIV) of the Bible uses it only three times (1 Chronicles 4:41; Galatians 1:7; Philippians 4:5). Even obscure words like "aforethought" show up more often. So, it's helpful to pause and spend some time meditating on the synonyms of "evident", which include "noticeable", "observable", and "recognisable". Other closely related words include "obvious" and "plain". The bottomline: "evident" means something others can see (see Matthew 5:16). Can others see your gentleness as a believer in Christ?

Secondly, "gentleness" isn't an everyday word, either. It appears only half a dozen times in the New Testament epistles (2 Corinthians 10:1; Galatians 5:23; Philippians 4:5; Colossians 3:12; 1 Timothy 6:11; 1 Peter 3:15). Elsewhere in the New Testament, it is always linked to other virtues. In one of the recorded instances where Jesus describes himself, He says, "I am gentle and humble in heart" (Matthew 11:29). In every way, Christ is completely gentle and humble. As Christians, we too are to be completely gentle and humble (Ephesians 4:2).

What does this look like to others? It looks like being patient, "bearing with one another in love" (v. 2), tolerance and reasonableness, care and consideration for others, mercy and kindness, and unselfishness and love. In a word, it looks like Jesus.

Several years ago, I realised I didn't always look like Jesus to my wife. Since then, I tell the Lord daily that I choose to honour, love, respect, cherish, nurture, and encourage Renée. I tell Him that I choose to be gentle and not exasperated, frustrated, harsh, contemptuous, demanding, or demeaning to her. That prayer revolutionised my marriage. Renée hasn't changed, but I sure have. As a result, we're both much happier, and others can see the difference.

Finally, we can't help looking and acting more like Jesus when we ponder the fact that "The Lord is near" (Philippians 4:5). Paul highlights the Lord's nearness, which speaks of the day of the Lord (see Day 11). It also speaks of the Lord's closeness to us.

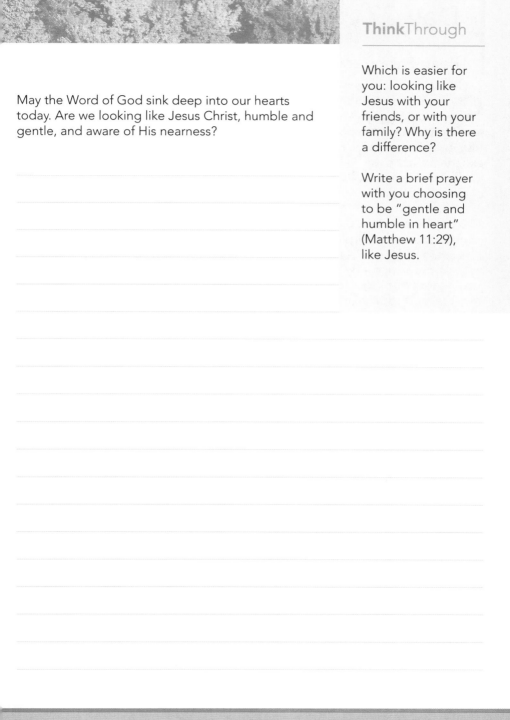

May the Word of God sink deep into our hearts today. Are we looking like Jesus Christ, humble and gentle, and aware of His nearness?

Which is easier for you: looking like Jesus with your friends, or with your family? Why is there a difference?

Write a brief prayer with you choosing to be "gentle and humble in heart" (Matthew 11:29), like Jesus.

Read Philippians 4:6

Some believers find this verse encouraging, while others don't. The difference lies in how they experience prayer. How can we experience it the way Paul describes it here? Let's consider each phrase of this verse in turn.

"**Do not be anxious . . .**" What is the answer to feelings of fear, concern, or anxiety? Paul tells us to stop worrying—by always praying with thanksgiving to God. Yes, it takes discipline. It calls for intentional recitation and meditation on this verse, especially in stressful circumstances. But, it works. When we desire reconciliation with a family member. When we wait on a key decision at church or work. When we lie still for a lengthy test in a hospital scanner or imager.

"**. . . about anything, but in every situation . . .**" Should we pray daily about whom we will meet? Paul says God wants us to pray "in every situation", so if it's in your heart and mind, pray about it. Yes, God already knows about it, but He wants you to lay it before Him humbly, in complete surrender. Jesus could have healed the blind, the leprous, and the deathly ill at the start of each new week. Instead, He waited to be asked. His question was, "What do you want me to do for you?" (see 1 Kings 3:5;

2 Chronicles 1:7; Matthew 20:32; Mark 10:36, 51; Luke 18:41). Imagine the Lord asking you that question. In a sense, He already has. How will you answer Him?

"**. . . by prayer and petition . . .**" Every day, I ponder on this: God the Father *loves* to hear prayers and petitions. First, the prayers of Jesus (Romans 8:34; Hebrews 7:25; 1 John 2:1). Second, the petitions of the Holy Spirit (Romans 8:26–27). Third, the prayers of believers in heaven (Revelation 5:8, 13; 6:9–11; 7:9–10; 8:3–4). Fourth, the petitions of our Christian family members, friends, and acquaintances on earth. Not only that, but God the Father also *loves* to answer these prayers, just as He answers mine. When we remember how God loves to hear our petitions and answer them, we're motivated to pray more.

"**. . . with thanksgiving, present your requests to God.**" As we go to God humbly, we cannot help thanking Him. After all, He is always at work in our midst (John 5:17). When we pray, therefore, we thank God in advance for His answers. Thanksgiving often inspires greater faith, hope, joy, and peace in our hearts. So thank God—often!

List previous answers to your prayers. Select one item from your list. Write a brief prayer of thanksgiving to God for His answer.

List what makes you anxious these days. Using Paul's model in today's verse, write a brief prayer about one item of concern.

Day 24

Read Philippians 4:7

It's hard to imagine meditating on Philippians 4:6 without including Philippians 4:7. Obeying the first will bring about the reward described in the second. And what a reward!

Prayer "in every situation" (v. 6) with thanksgiving to God brings about the reward of "the peace of God, which transcends all understanding" (v. 7). This peace arises not because we're in control, have a plan, or figured out all the options. It's not something we think, will, or create. Instead, it's God's peace, which is instant, tangible, and above all, supra-rational, meaning it is above and beyond reason. We find ourselves resting in the Lord, who imparts a peace the world can't comprehend, let alone replicate.

Take a moment to thank God daily for His infinite mystery: His knowledge, insight, understanding, wisdom, and ways. The Lord declares: "As the heavens are higher than the earth, so are my ways higher than your ways and my thoughts than your thoughts" (Isaiah 55:9). How good that we don't have to understand something in order to rest assured that God does—and to experience His peace.

Paul says the peace of God will "guard your hearts and your minds" (Philippians 4:7). The world, the flesh, and the devil want nothing more than to entice, distract, and contaminate our hearts and minds. Solomon advises in Proverbs 4:23, "Above all else, guard your heart, for everything you do flows from it". Yet, tragically, he let his own guard down, walked away from the Lord, and worshipped despicable idols (1 Kings 11:1–11). Almost every other good king of Judah let down his guard as well (the only exception was King Jotham, see 2 Chronicles 27:1–9).

However, let's not feel defeated or discouraged. We can be assured that God constantly searches us (Psalm 7:9; 139:23–24; Revelation 2:23). What's more, He has placed His new covenant (testament)—the life-changing gospel—in our hearts and minds (Jeremiah 31:33; Hebrews 8:10; 10:16). Best of all? The Spirit of Jesus Christ has come to dwell within us (Philippians 1:19; Romans 8:11) and always longs to fill us (Acts 13:52; Ephesians 5:18). In turn, His filling produces good fruit (Romans 15:13; Galatians 5:22–23), including love, joy, and peace.

It may seem hard to hold on to God's peace in the midst of difficult or chaotic circumstances. Still, let us draw hope and strength from the knowledge of who God is, what He has done for us in Christ Jesus, and what the Spirit continues to do in us.

ThinkThrough

Based on what we've seen in Philippians 4:6–7, how does one entrust something to God and attain His peace?

Describe a time when you experienced God's transcending peace in a memorable way.

Read Philippians 4:8

If we've asked God to guard our hearts and minds in Christ Jesus, what should we think about? The answer Paul gives in today's verse perfectly describes Jesus Christ. And it perfectly describes the Bible.

Thinking about God's written Word (Scripture) and incarnate Word (Jesus) may sound easy enough, but it's actually quite a challenge.

It's one thing to *know* about something. It's quite another to *love* someone. Before his Damascus road conversion (Acts 9:1–31), Saul knew the Hebrew Scriptures better than most of his peers, but he hated Jesus with a vengeance. After his conversion, what a change of heart!

Many Christians have favourite books of the Bible, stories about Jesus, or sermons. Favourites are fine as long as we don't neglect the rest. It's not enough to read God's Word here and there, or only once through. Many pastors and teachers recommend reading three chapters a day, which allows you to read God's Word cover to cover in a year. Occasionally, I'll set aside a year to read the New Testament four times. We must never neglect the Gospels, which compel us to fall ever more in love with our Lord and Saviour.

People often say they loved someone once in the past. It's entirely different to love someone steadfastly, faithfully, daily, forever. After one of Jesus' most controversial sermons, "many of his disciples turned back and no longer followed him" (John 6:26–66). When He then turned to the Twelve and asked if they also wanted to leave, Peter replied, "Lord, to whom shall we go? You have the words of eternal life. We have come to believe and to know that you are the Holy One of God" (vv. 67–69).

Yes, it's possible for our hearts to grow cold at times. As we see from Philippians 4:6–7, the solution is to talk to God about it, present our requests to Him, and thank Him for His answer to come. There have been times when, after I committed my request to God, His answer came the very next morning, causing me to laugh out loud. Why didn't I talk it over with God sooner? Indeed, we are reminded by today's verse and from personal experience that there is no need to look further than God's Word and Jesus. May our love for God's Word and Jesus grow and grow.

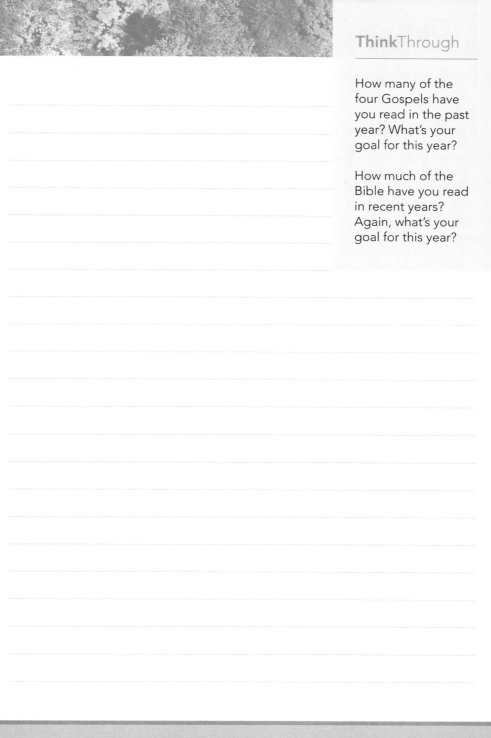

ThinkThrough

How many of the four Gospels have you read in the past year? What's your goal for this year?

How much of the Bible have you read in recent years? Again, what's your goal for this year?

Day 26

Read Philippians 4:9–12

In today's verses, Paul bares his heart of love and thanksgiving for the Philippians. He also encourages them to follow his example in being content in every circumstance.

First, Paul urges them to consider his life and teachings. By putting them into practice, he says, "the God of peace will be with you" (Philippians 4:9). This is the second great way to experience God's peace, coming on the heels of Paul's instructions to pray with thanksgiving (vv. 6–7).

Second, Paul expresses his joy for the gifts from the Philippians, brought by Epaphroditus. The gifts showed that "you renewed your concern for me" (v. 10). Paul quickly adds that he knew they had always been concerned, but for years didn't have a way to show it.

Third, Paul states two sides of the same coin. On one hand, he denies writing the previous verse because of need. On the other, he affirms that, "I have learned to be content whatever the circumstances" (v. 11).

Like other Pharisees, Saul (Paul's Jewish name) was probably a wealthy man who loved money (see Luke 16:14). As an apostle, however, Paul repeatedly lost his possessions to theft, riots, imprisonment, and shipwreck. As a result, "I have known hunger and thirst and have often gone without food; I have been cold and naked" (2 Corinthians 11:23–27). Therefore, Paul consistently worked hard to provide for his own needs and those of others (Acts 18:3; Ephesians 4:28; 1 Thessalonians 4:11–12; 2 Thessalonians 3:6–15).

This is not theory. Paul lived it out—for decades. My wife and I have, too. Due to an unprecedented financial collapse in the United States and the unjust actions of three corporations, we lost everything: our company, accumulated wealth, and home. But we had already memorised, meditated on, and applied these four verses. As a result, we weren't consumed by anxiety, anger, or bitterness. Instead, we experienced deep contentment throughout that experience and its aftermath. What Paul lived out, we can too.

It's clear that Paul isn't against wealth: "I know what it is to be in need, and I know what it is to have plenty. I have learned the secret of being content in any and every situation, whether well fed or hungry, whether living in plenty or in want" (Philippians 4:12). Like him, we experience deep contentment when our daily focus is worshipping, obeying, and living for the Lord.

If I could give one gift to every Christian, it would be this conviction: "Godliness with contentment is great gain" (1 Timothy 6:6).

Godliness is thanking God for who He is and living with the conviction that He is enough. In this context, what does "enough" mean to you?

Do you know anyone who has demonstrated godly contentment over the years? What has their example taught you?

Read Philippians 4:13

When taken out of context, what Paul says in today's verse can and has been misused countless times. Business leaders and motivational speakers love to quote it. It's been called one of the Bible's most inspirational verses. And it is. However, as with any verse, we need to keep our eyes firmly fixed on what's always true: God and His Word. The immediate meaning is finding contentment in the Lord in every circumstance. With that in mind, let's unpack this verse's meaning.

In His infinite sovereignty, God has unlimited power. We would do well to remember this with every sunrise, sunset, and starlit night. Our sun is but one of hundreds of billions of stars in one of hundreds of billions of galaxies placed across nearly 100 billion light years of space. God is the one who created them all and set each one in its place. He knows each star's name. *That* God, the LORD, the Creator of the heavens and earth, possesses infinite power. *He* can do everything.

The Lord wants us to do much. Yet without Him, we can do nothing (John 15:5). **To do anything of eternal worth, therefore, God needs to dwell in us and we need to pray for His will to be done (vv. 7–17).**

In context, today's verse means that Paul—and we—can overcome any and all of life's difficulties, accomplish God's will, and experience contentment, all because of Jesus' power at work in and through us.

We should never dare claim to wield, control, or possess the power of God ourselves. Philip, John, and Peter met a man who does just that in the city of Samaria. His given name is Simon, but he loves to be called "the Great Power of God" (Acts 8:10). When he asks to buy some of the Holy Spirit's power, Peter rebukes him in the harshest of terms (vv. 18–24).

Paul, too, meets another man like this in the city of Paphos. His given name is Bar-Jesus, though some call him "Elymas the sorcerer" (13:8). He actively opposes the missionary work of Barnabas and Paul, who rebukes Bar-Jesus in the harshest of terms and leaves him temporarily blind (vv. 9–12).

In contrast, we have the example of Ananias. Initially, he feels powerless to do what God commands (9:13–14). At times, we may feel this way too—that is, until we remember who indwells and empowers us: No less than God, the LORD, the Creator of the heavens and earth, who longs to work in and through us.

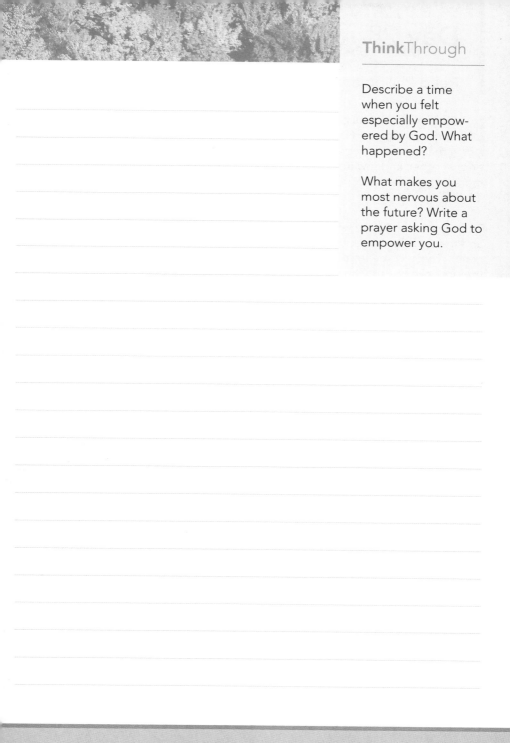

Describe a time when you felt especially empowered by God. What happened?

What makes you most nervous about the future? Write a prayer asking God to empower you.

Day 28

In today's verses, Paul blesses the Philippian believers. He talks about how their generosity produces eternal riches and rewards, "that more be credited to your account" (Philippians 4:17).

Throughout the New Testament, Jesus and the apostles speak about eternal riches. These come from God through the gospel of Jesus Christ, and are ours to enjoy—now and for all eternity.

Jesus also speaks of the folly of storing up wealth on earth. Instead, He offers "true riches" (Luke 16:11). Picking up on this, Paul too speaks of "the riches of God's grace", "the riches of his glorious inheritance in his holy people", "the incomparable riches of his grace, expressed in his kindness to us in Christ Jesus", "the boundless riches of Christ", and "his glorious riches" (Ephesians 1:7, 18; 2:7; 3:8, 16). He also describes the "glorious riches" and "full riches" of the gospel of Christ (Colossians 1:27; 2:2).

The apostles and the ascended Lord Jesus also speak about crowns. These eternal rewards are real, God-given, gospel-based, and to be treasured above anything on earth.

In one of his earlier epistles, Paul spoke of "a crown that will last for ever" (1 Corinthians 9:25). In his final epistle, Paul speaks of "the crown of righteousness, which the Lord, the righteous Judge, will award to me on that day—and not only to me, but also to all who have longed for his appearing" (2 Timothy 4:8).

Peter, too, goes on to promise that "when the Chief Shepherd appears, you will receive the crown of glory that will never fade away" (1 Peter 5:4). James speaks of "the crown of life that the Lord has promised to those who love him" (James 1:12). And the ascended Lord promises: "Be faithful, even to the point of death, and I will give you life as your victor's crown" (Revelation 2:10).

So, what kinds of generosity will be "credited to your account" (Philippians 4:17) in heaven?

They include financial gifts and other tangible aid to the poor, the needy, and the Lord's servants. Jesus says, "If anyone gives even a cup of cold water to one of these little ones who is my disciple, truly I tell you, that person will certainly not lose their reward" (Matthew 10:42). In addition, they include unspecified "righteous acts of God's holy people" (Revelation 19:8).

In the end, the what isn't as important as who does it for whom (and Whom). Therefore, do everything in Jesus' name for His honour and praise.

ThinkThrough

Can you describe a
time when you were
on the receiving end
of a righteous act?

Describe another
time when you acted
and blessed another
believer.

Read Philippians 4:18–19

n these two verses, Paul continues blessing the Philippian believers. First, he confirms receipt of their generous gifts: "I have received full payment and have more than enough; I am amply supplied, now that I have received from Epaphroditus the gifts you sent" (Philippians 4:18). The phrase "have more than enough" suggests that Epaphroditus added a personal donation atop the gifts that the church officially sent.

Second, Paul describes these gifts with beautiful words of worship: "They are a fragrant offering, an acceptable sacrifice, pleasing to God" (v. 18). Knowing the Old Testament very well and breathing its vocabulary, Paul refers to the sacred incense offered to the Lord in the tabernacle and temple. The burning incense created a very pleasant fragrance. The gifts from the Philippians are precious and beautiful, not just to Paul, but also to God.

As always, the Lord is our supreme example: "And live a life of love, just as Christ loved us and gave himself up for us as a fragrant offering and sacrifice to God" (Ephesians 5:2).

Accordingly, Peter calls us "a holy priesthood, offering spiritual sacrifices acceptable to God through Jesus Christ" (1 Peter 2:5). Paul affirms that "anyone who serves Christ in this way [of righteousness, peace and joy in the Holy Spirit] is pleasing to God" (Romans 14:17–18). Elsewhere, he adds: "Therefore, I urge you, brothers and sisters, in view of God's mercy, to offer your bodies as a living sacrifice, holy and pleasing to God—this is your true and proper worship" (12:1).

Third, Paul offers a final promise to the generous Philippian church: "And my God will meet all your needs according to the riches of his glory in Christ Jesus" (Philippians 4:19). This promise is collective, yet personal. It echoes the words of the Lord Jesus in His Sermon on the Mount: "So do not worry, saying, 'What shall we eat?' or 'What shall we drink?' or 'What shall we wear?' For the pagans run after all these things, and your heavenly Father knows that you need them. But seek first his kingdom and his righteousness, and all these things will be given to you as well" (Matthew 6:31–33).

Our generous giving blesses others and is a pleasing sacrifice to God. In turn, God promises to supply all of our needs, "according to the riches of his glory in Christ Jesus" (Philippians 4:19).

When receiving a generous gift, how do you prefer to thank the giver?

When you feel God leading you to offer a generous gift, what helps you to not worry? How does God feel about your sacrificial offerings?

Day 30

Read Philippians 4:20–23

It's time for Paul to offer a doxology, greetings, and a final blessing to his dear brothers and sisters in Christ from the city of Philippi.

First, his doxology: "To our God and Father be glory for ever and ever. Amen" (Philippians 4:20). As with his doxologies in other epistles, Paul gives honour and glory to God the Father. The same is true of the doxologies in Hebrews, 1 Peter, Jude, and Revelation. While our worship properly begins with God the Father, this doesn't mean we don't praise Jesus Christ and the Holy Spirit. We thank God the Father for sending His Son and express equal thanks for the Spirit. Indeed, each Sunday, countless millions of Christians around the world sing:

Praise God from whom all blessings flow;
Praise him, all creatures here below;
Praise him above, ye heavenly host:
Praise Father, Son, and Holy Ghost.

Second, Paul offers a series of three greetings. He begins with: "Greet all God's people in Christ Jesus" (v. 21), which refers to all believers associated with the church in Philippi. He continues with: "The brothers and sisters who are with me send greetings" (v. 21), which refers to Timothy, Epaphroditus, and others. And he concludes with: "All God's people here send you greetings, especially those who belong to Caesar's household" (v. 22). This refers to Christians in the city where Paul is imprisoned, and includes those won to Jesus Christ through his own witness (1:13, 14, 16).

Now that travel between cities and nations is more prevalent than ever, we should remember Paul's example. When we arrive in a new place, let's greet our brothers and sisters in Christ. Let's give them the greetings of believers from our home city (and nation). **Such greetings bind us together in Christian love and offer a powerful witness to a watching world.**

Finally, Paul offers a benediction. In many ways, Paul's benedictions serve as bookends to his opening salutations. With two exceptions (1 & 2 Timothy), the latter are nearly identical in his epistles: "Grace and peace to you from God our Father and the Lord Jesus Christ" (Philippians 1:2). With two exceptions (in Romans and Ephesians), and a little bit more variety, his benedictions offer the same blessing: "The grace of the Lord Jesus Christ be with your spirit. Amen" (4:23).

Whenever we meet fellow believers, we do well to close with a similar benediction. It blesses all present and brings honour, glory, and praise to our Lord and Saviour.

In Christian gatherings, which of these—doxology, greetings, benediction—have you heard, and how often?

After journeying through Paul's epistle to the Philippians, what do you most want to remember?

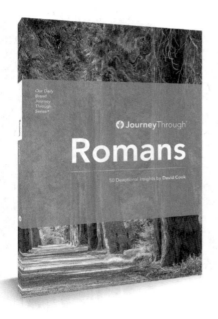

Journey Through

Romans

The book of Romans outlines what Christians believe, and explains God's perfect plan in bringing sinners back to Him. More than any other single book in the whole of the Bible, it has played a crucial role in shaping church history. It has been called the greatest theological document ever written. But precisely for the same reason, many have found it a daunting book to study. They ask, "Will I be able to grasp the difficult concepts in this book?" Yes, you can! David Cook writes in a style that makes difficult truths easy to understand. Rediscover why the gospel is such good news and walk away with a deeper appreciation of what and why you believe.

David Cook was Principal of the Sydney Missionary and Bible College for 26 years. He is an accomplished writer and has authored Bible commentaries, books on the Minor Prophets, and several Bible study guides.

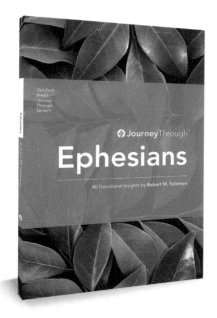

Journey Through

Ephesians

Paul's epistle to the Ephesians celebrates God's eternal plan to bless us and marvels at Christ's salvation work. It not only offers a theological and pastoral reflection on the church and its nature, origin, character, mission, and future, but also poses us the challenge to live faithfully as children of light.

Discover what Ephesians says about the blessings that the triune God has given to the church, the gospel mystery that it has been entrusted with, and how the church is to live out its identity and calling.

Robert M. Solomon served as Bishop of The Methodist Church in Singapore from 2000–2012. He has an active itinerant preaching and teaching ministry in Singapore and abroad. He is the author of more than 30 books, including *The Race*, *The Conscience*, *The Sermon of Jesus*, *Faithful to the End*, *Finding Rest for the Soul*, and *God in Pursuit*.

Journey Through

Hosea

As God's spokesman, Hosea is told by Him to marry Gomer, a prostitute, and to go again and again to woo her back despite her many infidelities. Hosea's commitment to love Gomer gives us a glimpse of God's love for us. God loves His people as passionately and as jealously as a devoted husband loves his wife. Even when we wander from Him and our hearts cool towards Him, He continues to come after us and to draw us back to Him. God's love will never let us go. Rekindle your love and commitment to the One who loves you!

David Gibb is the former Vicar of St. Andrew's Church in Leyland and Honorary Canon of Blackburn Cathedral. He is committed to training church planters and gospel workers, and is one of the contributors to a new NIV Study Bible. He is also author of a book on Revelation.

For information on our resources, visit **ourdailybread.org**. Alternatively, please contact the office nearest you from the list below, or go to **ourdailybread.org/locations** for the complete list of offices.

BELARUS
Our Daily Bread Ministries
PO Box 82, Minsk, Belarus 220107
belarus@odb.org • (375-17) 2854657; (375-29) 9168799

GERMANY
Our Daily Bread Ministries e.V.
Schulstraße 42, 79540 Lörrach
deutsch@odb.org • +49 (0) 7621 9511135

IRELAND
Our Daily Bread Ministries
64 Baggot Street Lower, Dublin 2, D02 XC62
ireland@odb.org • +353 (0) 1676 7315

RUSSIA
MISSION Our Daily Bread
PO Box "Our Daily Bread",
str.Vokzalnaya 2, Smolensk, Russia 214961
russia@odb.org • 8(4812)660849; +7(951)7028049

UKRAINE
Christian Mission Our Daily Bread
PO Box 533, Kiev, Ukraine 01004
ukraine@odb.org • +380964407374; +380632112446

UNITED KINGDOM (Europe Regional Office)
Our Daily Bread Ministries
PO Box 1, Millhead, Carnforth, LA5 9ES
europe@odb.org • +44 (0)15395 64149

ourdailybread.org

Sign up to *Journey Through*

We would love to support you with the *Journey Through* series! Please be aware we can only provide one copy of each future *Journey Through* book per reader (previous books from the series are available to purchase).

If you know of other people who would be interested in this series, we can send you introductory *Journey Through* booklets to pass onto them (which include details on how they can easily sign up for the books themselves).

☐ **I would like to regularly receive the *Journey Through* series**

☐ **Please send me ____ copies of the *Journey Through* introductory booklet**

Just complete and return this sign up form to us at:

Our Daily Bread Ministries, PO Box 1, Millhead, Carnforth, LA5 9ES, United Kingdom

Here at Our Daily Bread Ministries we take your privacy seriously. We will only use this personal information to manage your account, and regularly provide you with *Journey Through* series books and offers of other resources, four ministry update letters each year, and occasional additional mailings with news that's relevant to you. We will also send you ministry updates and details of Our Daily Bread Publishing products by email if you agree to this. In order to do this we share your details with our UK-based mailing house and Our Daily Bread Ministries in the US. We do not sell or share personal information with anyone for marketing purposes.

Please do not complete and sign this form for anyone but yourself. You do not need to complete this form if you already receive regular copies of *Journey Through* from us.

Full Name (Mr/Mrs/Miss/Ms): _____

Address: _____

_____

Postcode: _____ Tel: _____

Email: _____
☐ I would like to receive email updates and details of Our Daily Bread Publishing products.

Signature: _____